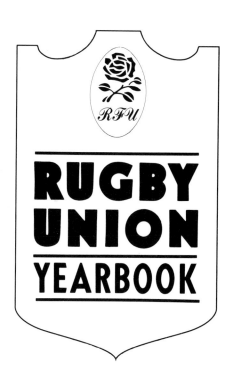

RUGBY UNION
YEARBOOK

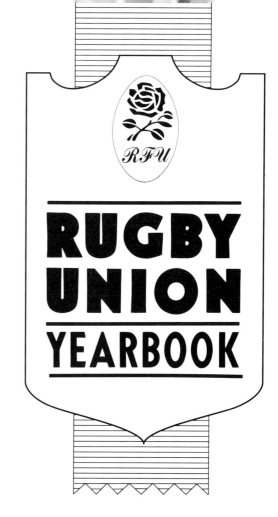

RUGBY UNION YEARBOOK

EDITED BY
MICK CLEARY

VIRGIN

optomen

Contents

 SPORTS EDITIONS LIMITED

Managing Director   Richard Dewing
Art Director   Mary Hamlyn
Designers   Sandra Cowell
                      Rob Kelland
Desk Editor   Leslie Smillie
Picture Research   Sandra Cowell
                      Rob Kelland

A Virgin/Optomen book
First published in Great Britain
in 1989 by
W H Allen & Co Plc
Sekforde House
175/9 St John Street
London EC1V 4LL

ISBN 1-85227-012-8

Produced, edited and designed by
Sports Editions Limited, 3 Greenlea Park, Prince George's Road, London SW19 2JD

Typeset in Palatino and Kabel
by Sports Editions Limited

Origination, printing and binding by
Butler & Tanner Ltd, Frome, Somerset

Cover originated and printed by
The Hartlebury Group Ltd, Hartlebury,
Nr Kidderminster, Worcestershire

Photograph of Gavin Hastings (opposite) by Russell Cheyne

From the President

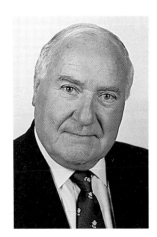

There were encouraging signs for English rugby throughout a season that began with a good win over Australia and ended with a resounding victory in Bucharest againgst Romania. In addition, the British Lions won the test series in Australia — all these events are well documented in this book.

It is easy to forget the many sporting moments which make up a season and I am sure it will give people great pleasure to sit down with this book and revive the memories of last season. I hope this inaugural venture will be successful and form part of a long-standing series.

Rugby Football is thriving at present. Our domestic competitions are now well established with the welcome support of our various sponsors. There has never been greater interest in the events staged at Twickenham but this is also typical of the club scene where crowds are growing, membership is strong, and youngsters continue to be attracted to the sport.

At international level we appear to be improving to a point whereby we can once again take our place among the leading rugby nations of the world. The dedication of our players and those who prepare them for the field of play is of the highest order and will lead to continuing success in the future.

May I wish you all a very successful and enjoyable season and happy reading.

D. L. Sanders
RFU President

Preface

What is an editor? A person who takes most of the glory and does little of the graft? So it seems to me after my first appearance at the top of the credits. Of course the glory has yet to come, but having spent many a happy hour reading, re-reading and then re-re-reading the contents of this book I am sure that acclaim will follow. It is of course the contributors who make or break a book such as this. If the content is flat and tedious then there is virtually nothing the editor can do about it — except not invite the writer to contribute next year of course.

There is a fine variety of writing and topics within these pages, ranging from reviews of the major competitions to more polemical pieces from David Kirk and Dudley Wood. It was a pleasure to have a woman contributing to the book — I am sure you will find Margaret McDonald's appraisal of the 1988 Wallaby tour perceptive as well as entertaining. Her work as a sports journalist in a male dominated world has not always been easy. One of her earlier jobs involved interviewing Peter Shilton in Australia after the soccer "test" match. After fighting her way past fans and security men she finally met him outside the dressing rooms. He saw the pen and notebook in her hand and, before she had a chance to speak, took them both and wrote "All the best, Peter Shilton."

We have tried to produce a challenging review of the year rather than a totally comprehensive one. Statistics only ever tell part of a story — it is the interpretation of the story which is often of most interest. I hope you enjoy this particular story.

Mick Cleary

Acknowledgements

Thanks are due to the following for their invaluable assistance in the production of this title: *The Independent* for permission to use Martin Johnson's article on Dusty Hare; the *Leicester Mercury* for final career statistics on Dusty Hare; Margaret McDonald for the Australian tour statistics; Roger Shackleton Associates for the Pilkington Cup results; Michael Humphries + Partners for the final standings in the Courage Clubs Championship; John Vivian of the *Surrey Comet* and Paul Beken for the London Welsh photographs; John Griffiths for his selection of archive material and the scoring records for Serge Blanco and David Campese; and Russell Cheyne for his help with the selection of photographs.

The fearsome French front row forwards prepare to scrum down against the Scots

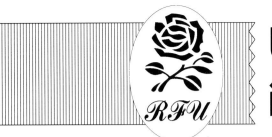

Ups and downs in the leagues

Robert Armstrong

All-conquering Bath had the 1989 Courage Clubs Championship sewn up well before Easter. The super-fit Avon club cast a long shadow over the English game, setting standards that will soon become the norm for any club that is serious about putting silverware in the trophy case. However, league rugby, still in its infancy, is having teething problems, and

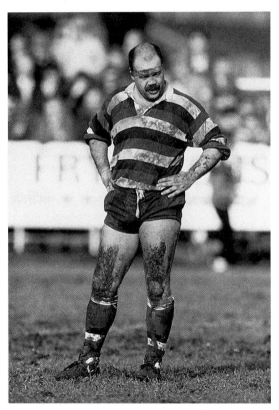

Gareth Chilcott was a major influence in Bath's most successful season ever

not every club believes the competition favours its special traditions. Here we find out how Jamie Salmon would streamline the First Division, why London Scottish feel bad luck cost them their place in the Second, and how men of ambition are keeping Rugby on the up and up.

DIVISION I

Every club player knows that the Courage leagues have hit English rugby like an invigorating blast of fresh air. The majority of teams are now fitter, sharper, and more competitive. Nowhere is this truer than in the First Division where league fixtures create a cup-tie atmosphere that intensifies local loyalties and stimulates attendances. Perhaps the most beneficial side-effect of league rugby is the improved performance of England's representative sides at the senior, B, student and Under-21 levels. Never before have the nation's leading players shown such a sustained degree of pride, motivation and durability. The collective habit of believing that results matter has given England a new sense of purpose.

Yet, like every new competition, the Courage Clubs Championship has to some extent been feeling its way. The bizarre decision to award each club one point merely for turning up was abandoned at the end of the 1987-88 season. Player movement between clubs has prompted greater vigilance over the eligibility rules and given rise to a pilot registration scheme in the south-west.

One man who believes there is room for further improvement is the former Harlequins, England and New Zealand centre Jamie Salmon, who recently retired from the game after he had enjoyed an outstanding season which won him a place in the England squad. Yet, at the early age of 29, he decided he was no longer prepared to make the rigorous commitment to training required nowadays for the first-class game: "You really have to give it everything to make

Jamie Salmon would like to see a play-off system to decide the promotion and relegation places in the leagues

Wade Dooley of Preston Grasshoppers... how long can this Area League North team hope to hold on to such a quality player?

seen a greater concentration of talent among the top half-dozen clubs but I think that is good for the game. After all, it is only when you get the best players competing against each other on a regular basis that the game develops consistently higher standards."

Conversely, Salmon argues that automatic relegation for the bottom two clubs in the division is "too harsh" because it offers no safety net for clubs who may still be better than those who gain promotion. He would prefer to see a play-off system introduced under which the top two in the Second Division would have to beat the relegation candidates in order to go up. "That would add more spice to the competition," he said.

Salmon believes that rugby can no longer be a fifteen- or seventeen-man game for clubs that desire success in leagues. Injuries and lack of availability means you need a good squad of at least twenty-five players to compete throughout the season. As the game becomes more commercial and more professional those clubs who stick to the letter of the amateur regulations will find it harder to keep together a squad of sufficient depth.

"Everyone knows who can or cannot win the championship now that the best players keep going to the same clubs. It has not been easy for Harlequins to build a squad with depth especially as there are now four London clubs out of twelve in the First Division. Obviously London has benefitted more than most from leagues." By the same token the North has suffered from leagues, with only one club, Orrell, left in the top flight. Clearly the priority the North has traditionally given to the county championship, the competing claims of Rugby League, and the drift of players to jobs in the south have all contributed to a weaker club structure which saw northern clubs Waterloo and Liverpool St Helens relegated to the Second Division last season.

sure your club does well in league matches," explained Salmon, who had his first experience of league rugby as an 18 year old in Auckland. "It would certainly suit the players if the season was better structured, for example, dropping the county and divisional championships would ease fixture congestion, though I don't think the powers-that-be have the guts to go that far."

"It is in the First Division, not the divisional competition, that national selectors will be looking for the kind of individual performances that show international potential. We have

Richard Hill of Bath gave much to his club's victory in the Courage Clubs Championship

The strong feelings of friendship at London Scottish mean that even top players such as Derek White will stick with the club as they attempt to bounce back from relegation

Salmon forecasts that smaller, unfashionable clubs will experience the greatest difficulty in retaining the loyalty of international players who become anxious about the perils of playing in a backwater. "For instance, I don't see how Preston Grasshoppers can hang on to Wade Dooley for very much longer," he said. Despite the pressures of league rugby which, says Salmon, "means players must adopt better attitudes," he would like to see a bigger First Division of, say, fifteen clubs playing fourteen (instead of eleven) games a season. "More league matches in the second half of the season would sustain public interest," he says, "but no matter how many fixtures you have, ambitious teams will have to develop quick ball skills, which means they must learn to ruck. Adopting the All Black style," says Salmon, "is the key to league success."

DIVISION II

League rugby proved to be a double-edged sword for London's three Exiles clubs in the Second Division last season. The Irish briefly flirted with trouble and, perverse as ever, ended up missing promotion by a whisker. The Scottish and the Welsh wore a brave face in early autumn, and then, like a bad Celtic double act, hit a long losing streak that duly ended in relegation.

The Welsh, who were London's pride in the early seventies, went quietly, with just a single victory. But there was sympathy for the Scots who suffered a stream of injuries, fell foul of the eligibility rules, and made an agonising exit, despite hammering high-flying Coventry in their final game.

Talk to last season's captain, Charlie Richardson, and you are likely to be persuaded that the league system was loaded against Scottish. "It is very difficult for an Exiles club to develop the true depth required in a first XV squad," said Richardson. "The fact that we have

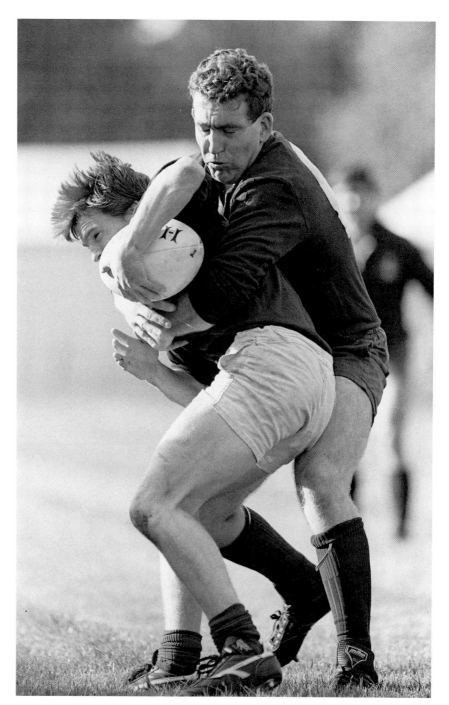

restricted membership by nationality is bound to limit the supply of good players coming into the club. Even so, we went down largely due to injuries at crucial times. The team did not warrant relegation and I think we will prove that in

London Scottish and Sudbury clash in the cup, and perhaps next season in the league?

ing me at the after dinner drinks in the upstairs bar with the words: "You must be Margaret." While at times I felt like a laboratory experiment at various functions, the players rarely commented on my uniqueness. Their main concern was having the showers hot and the beer cold in the dressing rooms rather than having a female journalist present.

After the Wallabies had demolished a South of Scotland side containing eight Test players 29 - 4 the week before the Murrayfield Test, I tracked down Lloyd Walker in the bath soaking off the soreness. He had played a magnificent distribution game at inside centre feeding passes to Michael Cook outside of him and working loop-arounds with Lynagh that drew gasps of pleasure from the grandstand. After the loss to London Division, one Fleet Street rugby writer said Walker was "aptly named" as his slowness around the field did not help Australia's chances of victory, but up in

Scotland he was literally bathing in the glory of a job well done, not in speed but in timing.

"I try not to read too much what you blokes write", Walker said as I sat crouched down beside him taking notes and feeling the overspill from the bath seeping into my skirt. Walker, to his credit, did not care or distinguish whether it was a man or woman talking to him while he was in the bath. I was just a journalist doing my job. Although I was constantly accused of stealing players' hotel keys, or of giving Damien Frawley his cold (I had mine first), I was never made to feel an outsider by the Wallaby party.

I turned 30 surrounded by 30 footballers who gave me hearty birthday-type slaps on my back as they came off the training field (the forwards hurt the most) and even a few kisses on the cheek. They were always gentlemen and international rugby players but they became people I could call friends first.

Nick Farr-Jones led his side to a victory over the Barbarians which was sparked by the brilliance of David Campese

Giants and giant killers in the cup

Barrie Fairall

A record fifth win in six years for mighty Bath in front of a record capacity crowd provided a clamorous climax to the club season at Twickenham where, after 18 years, English rugby's knock-out competition came of age as Stuart Barnes raised aloft the new Pilkington Cup. In a hard and competitive final so much in keeping with the modern game it had been an occasion of emotional highs, the people's favourite Dusty Hare giving Leicester a slender lead with two penalties from his trusty boot and Barnes replying in kind before snatching victory with a dramatic late try.

But if Bath and Leicester earned the applause as current-day giants then it was Berry Hill and Aspatria who won recognition for their giant-killing roles in another season which served to illustrate the impact of a league structure. There were times when the senior gate-taking clubs were spared the embarrassment of a soccer style cup upset but now nothing is certain when venturing, for example, into the Forest of Dean and the depths of Cumbria and the signs are that trips such as these will become increasingly fraught with danger.

For London Welsh, the blushes were still lingering from the previous season's defeat at the hands of Berry Hill, who had come away smiling from the Old Deer Park with a 13 - 10 win in the third round. Now the luck of the

**Stuart Barnes of
Bath lines up a
penalty in the final**

Preedy of Gloucester, who lost out to Bath by two penalties to one in the semi-final

By now the Forest was echoing to the sounds of heroic deeds, Berry Hill having already accounted for another National Division side, Askelans from the Third, in the first round. It was then, beaming with post-match pleasure, that the Berry Hill captain Jeff Powell looked the guests in the eye and said: "We enjoyed stuffing you." Askeans had to grin and bear it, much like the Welsh later, while round about the same time Lydney were experiencing similar feelings. Local rivals of Berry Hill, they had travelled to meet Finchley, the Middlesex Cup holders who were three rungs down the league ladder, and lost out by a single point. For Finchley, like so many others, the leagues have brought them to life. Garnet Edwards, the club coach, says: "The players were disillusioned with a set up that lacked direction, so we introduced a vastly different coaching approach and injected new vitality into the club."

Finchley fell at the second hurdle at home to Richmond and Berry Hill at the third in a Sunbury meeting with London Irish but the giant-killing continued as Aspatria reached the fourth round with a stunning 6 - 3 victory over First Division Moseley, whose game plan appeared to be nothing more subtle than attempting to scrummage the Cumbrians into the Irish Sea. Well, Aspatria stood their ground — Bower Park by name, compact by nature — and stand-off Andrew Harrison did the rest with a penalty and dropped goal. Aspatria then prayed for another home tie, as did Havant after being steered home with a match-winning try from captain Andy Perry in the tie against Exeter.

In the event both lost out. Aspatria were drawn away to Wasps, whom they had run close the previous season in the third round at Bower Park, Havant were sent to Wakefield, and by the end of the day Wakefield stood alone as the only non First Division side to reach the quarter finals. But the giant-killing was over for another season, Wakefield were unable to

draw had produced the same pairing, though the cruel twist was that it was poor Welsh who would have to do the visiting. "Actually," says the Berry Hill spokesman Geoff Goddard, "we prefer playing the first class clubs." How true, because once again the Welsh fell apart. In hostile territory they were given a frosty reception by the Berry Hill stand-off Peter Hoare, who landed six penalties in his side's 24 - 9 triumph.

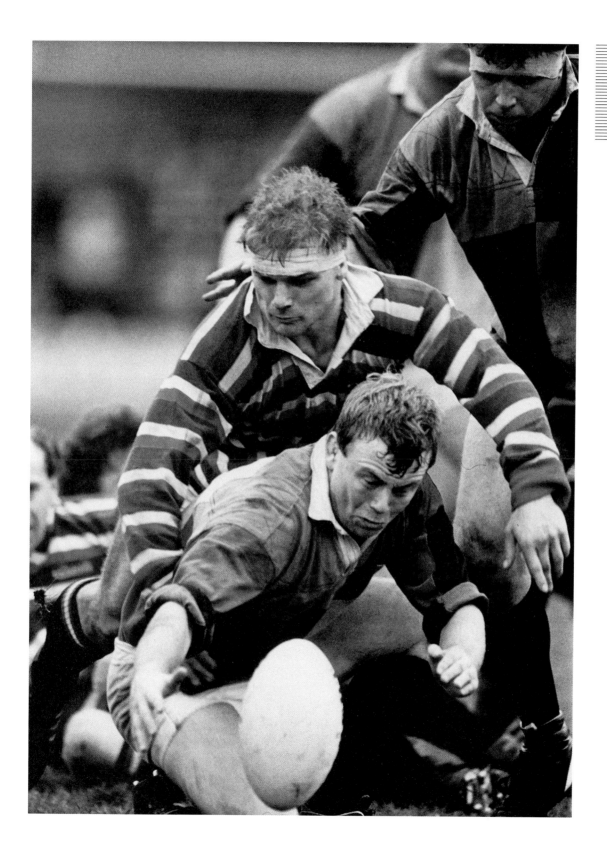

Victory over Harlequins in the semi-final provided Leicester's Dusty Hare with the ideal venue as the send-off to his career

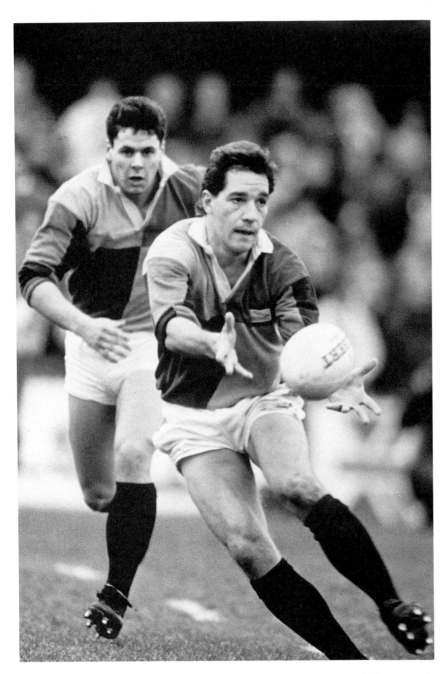

Jamie Salmon
ended up on the
losing side as
Leicester beat
Harquelins 16 - 7

Recreation Ground with a 78th minute try from the irrepressible Richard Hill.

And so it was down to the nitty-gritty, each semi-final a sell out in a season of soaring attendances. At Kingsholm, there was an expectant air about the proceedings. Bath, the newly crowned League Champions, were looking forward to a first Cup and League double but blurring their vision stood Gloucester, who the previous month had brought to an end the unbeaten run of their great West Country rivals. It was bound to be a close and hard fought encounter, though scoring-wise the issue was settled before the break when Barnes answered a Tim Smith penalty with two match-winners of his own. "We'll celebrate tonight," said the Bath captain, "and then we'll begin to think about Leicester."

The Tigers themselves had been painting the town, the Cusworth/Hare show beginning early at The Stoop after Stuart Thresher had put the holders Harlequins in front with a penalty. Cusworth kicked left and Hare came up to gather the ball and enjoy a stroll to the corner. Cusworth then sent Aadel Kardooni on a run to the posts for Hare to convert and, after Richard Cramb had scored a try for Quins, Cusworth completed his afternoon's work with a party-piece dropped goal. Hare's penalty rounded off the proceedings and Leicester and their hordes of supporters were once again Twickenham bound.

There, to the delight of the RFU, not to mention Pilkington in their very first year of Cup sponsorship, the house full signs went up. Yes, the competition had come of age and what a send off for the retiring Hare. "Hare today, gone tomorrow" read one newspaper headline in a glowing tribute to the maestro and if there was to be no fairytale ending to a glittering career for the greatest goalkicker the game has ever seen then it was simply because Bath had emerged as the greatest team in the land.

suppress the ruthless efficiency of Gloucester's pack at College Grove, and the giants were left to fight out their own battles in the semi-finals once the holders Harlequins had disposed of Nottingham, the Les Cusworth-tuned Leicester had out-driven Wasps, and Bath had pulled the plug on Bristol in a glorious mudlark at the

Wakefield in1923 after captaining Cambridge to victory over Oxford, the RAF to victory in the Inter-Services tournament, and leading the England pack to victory in all four internationals played

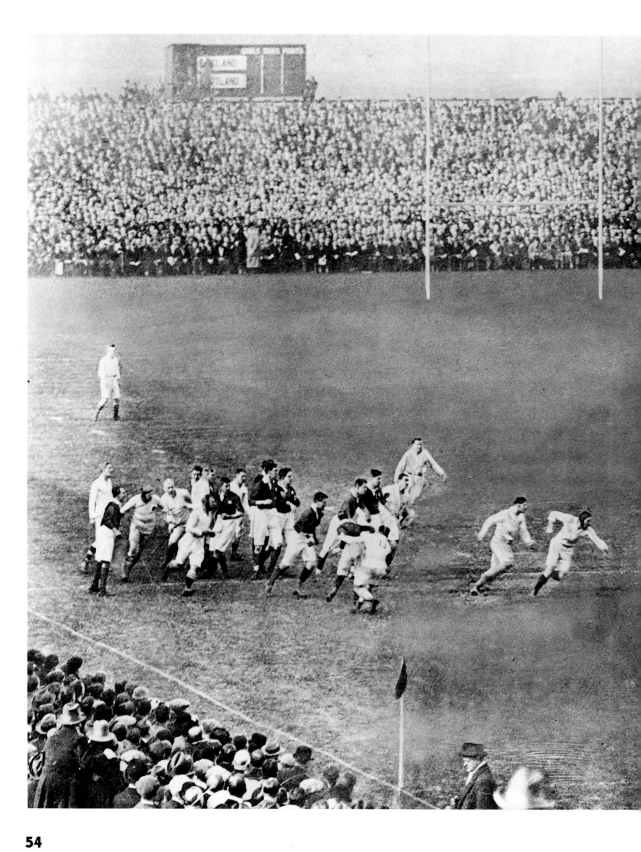

England v Scotland at Twickenham before a record crowd in 1924: England's 19 - 0 victory gave them the championship for the sixth time in ten seasons

Wakefield, referee
T. H. Vale and
Scotland captain
J. C. R. Buchanan
before the 1924
Calcutta Cup match

Harquelins, wrote of him: "Certainly he had all the physical attributes required to make a great forward. He was exceedingly powerful, thickly and compactly built, though he was a big man and weighed over 14 stone stripped. He was always in the thick of the battle but he was never hurt. Everything about him was as solid as the trunk of a tree... and in addition to his strength he was exceptionally fast and could overhaul most wing three-quarters."

"Wakefield in full cry for the line was a formidable proposition indeed for the defence, and since he could run and handle the ball as well as any three-quarter, or control the ball in a dribble like Stanley Matthews, he was that rare thing, a complete footballer. Not only did he set a tremendous example of relentless hostility and aggression but his fighting spirit was never subdued or depressed by disaster. Wakefield, however, was not merely a remarkably gifted player. Like Vassall and Stoop he studied the game in the closest detail, analysing his opponents and their methods before a match, and going over every phase of play afterwards so that no lesson might be lost."

That last point was well illustrated in the 1922 Varsity match when his plan for undermining Oxford, unexpected winners the year before, had a machiavellian quality. It was to allow Oxford to take the ball as they liked in the opening quarter of an hour, so giving Cambridge the chance repeatedly to hit the dangerous Oxford centres and knock them off their game. The ploy worked, and so did Wakefield's deployment of the back row, the hallmark of his play, in closing defensive gaps near the scrum and in midfield attacking with the ball kicked in from the wings. Cambridge won 21 - 8.

If Wakefield was eulogised by his contemporaries as a player, a leader and an innovator, his roll of honour gives this credence. The future captain of England also led Sedbergh — the school which shaped his severe though less than spartan values, the RAF, Cambridge, Middlesex and Harlequins. His record of England caps stood for 40 years before Budge Rogers surpassed him with 34.

Wakefield left the RAF to go into business and for nearly 30 years, too, he was a Conservative MP, first for Swindon then Marylebone. His toryism was deeply rooted but in rugby, as in other things, he was what we would now call a radical Tory. Within certain fixed beliefs he was enthusiastic for experiment and change. At Sedbergh, for instance, it was an article of faith that forwards should never heel the ball in their own half. "But when I got into top football with the Harlequins," he once told me (in 1969, when he was 71), "and talked over things with Adrian Stoop, we completely reversed all that. So the time when we used the wheel was in attack and in our own half we heeled. Then by a quick heel we could either clear our line or start a movement to score ... the defence was dislocated and that was how we scored tries against the invincible All Blacks."

What he wanted to conserve was the spirit of the game (contravened, in his view, when a match was on penalties) and its amateurism. He felt the RFU's proper business was with the Commonwealth, leaving the French to look after the continent and with the other burgeoning rugby countries kept at arms length. Perhaps he would have been won round to the World Cup, but at that time he was fearful of rugby developing into an international sport like soccer. He deplored the spate of new legislation: "In my days, provided you were onside you could do almost anything you liked, pack anywhere in the scrum, bind how you wished. Now it's all laid down in a quite frightful way."

On the other hand he was far in advance of his time in wanting to curb touch kicking as a means of gaining ground. Nearly 40 years before the quaintly named "Australian dispensation" became universal, Wakefield was arguing that when and where the ball was kicked out of play, the other side, instead of having to contest a lineout, should be free to kick it or pass it unhindered. Now, since there were to be lineouts, he saw no good reason why players should be penalised for lifting. If that was the most efficient way of winning the ball, so be it. Wakefield was a man of principle but also of refreshing common sense.

PRINCE ALEXANDER OBOLENSKY

Half a century or more before the USSR emerged as a rugby power capable of beating France (admittedly on a bad day), one Russian, admittedly a White Russian, not a Red, enjoyed an enduring hour of glory at Twickenham. He was Prince Alexander Obolensky who on 4th January 1936 joined that select band who have had a try named after them. In his brief career he scored many tries, of course, but the one that is remembered as Obolensky's try, his second that afternoon, stands apart from all the rest.

That he came to be playing for England at all that day is some sort of testimony to the British knack for absorbing foreign bodies and making them their own. Obolensky was born in Petrograd (now Leningrad) in 1916, the son of Prince Alexis Obolensky, an officer of the Tsar's Imperial Horse Guard. One year later, when the revolution came, this was no longer a position of privilege and the young prince was sent to England for safety. There he was sent to Trent

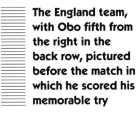
The England team, with Obo fifth from the right in the back row, pictured before the match in which he scored his memorable try

switched from the more traditional toe-punting method, and 15 years later Hare was converting a try to overtake Doble's world record of 3,651 points on the former Moseley full-back's own club ground. Seven years on and Hare has virtually doubled it.

Hare set records throughout a career spanning virtually two decades, not least in managing to get himself dropped five times by his country. He was about to be jettisoned for the sixth time in 1985 when he asked England not to bother him again ("I think that's when I started enjoying my rugby most of all"), by which time he had won a record 25 caps at full-back and scored — despite not being the kicker in his first two internationals — a record 240 points for his country.

He was about to break his own club record of 396 points in a season in 1988 before dropping a five-bar gate on his big toe down on his Nottinghamshire farm. He claims that records were never a huge motivator and he would almost certainly like to be remembered more for being a bloody good full-back than a goal-kicking machine. Hare's contribution to the brilliant running rugby pioneered by Leicester in the late seventies was crucial, and it was largely because the Hare explosion into the line became a phut that the Tigers ceased to mesmerise opposing defences as much as before.

As the English do not traditionally warm to infallibility, Hare is better loved for being prone to the occasional unbelievable howler. "An errant genius," says his former Leicester coach Chalky White. "Never predictable," recalling the time Hare won a "superstars" tournament among Nottingham's leading sportsmen at Trent Bridge, despite the embarrassment of losing the goal-kicking competition to cricketer Clive Rice.

We like our heroes modest, too, which is why Hare's speech went down so well when a tree was planted in his honour in his home

In his final season for Leicester he set a new club record of 438 points

village of South Clifton. He dedicated the monument to the local canine population who, he says, "never miss a chance to pay their respects." White says: "His records are far less important to me than the man. His head is the same size as when he came in." It's tough to get an inflated opinion of yourself at Leicester, where news of Hare's MBE in the New Year's Honours list was conveyed to a team-mate. "Must stand for," he said after due reflection, "Member of the Bald 'Eaded Society."

The season in pictures

Russell Cheyne

What lifts a rugby picture, like any other sports picture, are the facial expressions. Here Mike Hall and Scott Hastings illustrate the point at the Scotland v Wales match in the 1989 Five Nations.

Allsport's Russell Cheyne was asked to make a selection of his favourite (Allsport) photos taken during the 1988-89 season — only after he had done so was he asked, much to his horror, to provide the captions to go along with his choice! Apart from pages 73 and 74 (by Allsport colleagues Simon Bruty and Dan Smith) all the pictures here are from Russell's files.

I think this is what mimics at rugby clubs would refer to as "a little bit of argy bargy in the line out." It's an area of play that has always been unclear to me as to what is allowed to happen — there are so many laws regarding the line-out that there could be a number of infringements at each one. I think that this picture by my Allsport colleague Simon Bruty shows at least one of them! (Cambridge University versus the Japanese touring side Doshisha University)

Neath versus Llanelli in the 1989 Schweppes Cup Final. A sell-out crowd at the Arms Park watch opposing wingers Alan Edmunds and Ieuan Evans in a commited challenge for the ball. There is a terrific atmosphere and the pre-match singing even affects the photographers on the pitch — leaving each with a lump in the throat and the hair standing on the back of the neck. Certainly no ordinary club match.

Robert Norster jumps clear in the line-out for Major Stanley's XV against Oxford University. Oxford seems tranquil with the church spires reddish in the low winter sun. It's cold and crisp, the gloves are on, and I'm looking for a picture in the first few minutes before the sun disappears behind the stands.

England's flying winger Rory Underwood (above). The RAF base is a completely different environment to the rugby training grounds I normally see Rory in — all high tech and beyond me. I'm left wondering how he has the time to play top class rugby as well. The first meeting of England and Romania at under-21 level in Bucharest, May 1989 (right).The Cathay Pacific Hong Kong Sevens (main picture)— the most colourful and exciting two days of rugby. A chance to see many different international teams.

Major Stanley's XV v Oxford University. At a scrum there are so many options it's difficult to photograph. Occasionally a flanker will pick up the ball and charge towards the camera and here John Hall fills the role perfectly. Just right for me, but I pity the poor guy who has to tackle him!

Will Carling, the England captain, on the banks of the River Thames — now the only part of the riverbank with clean railings as we spent about 10 minutes cleaning off bird droppings! I was worried about Will's suit as he had to stand perfectly still for about 15 seconds for each exposure and became a target for passing seagulls.

Blanco & Campese:
a dazzling duo

Steve Jones

Who would be an artist in this era? At the moment so many rugby teams at the top level are grappling with the problems of ferocious pressure defence, the ogre of the age. A great, moving, thumping wall which descends on any team in any international or major club or tour match. If the teams are fairly evenly matched up front then, too often, individual flair is turned off. So many of the matches in the 1989 Five Nations championship for example were won by the defensive monster and by the sheer animal conviction of the play.

So how do Blanco and Campo do it? How can they stand out from the fuss and the fury and shine brilliantly, not just occasionally but season after season? How can they keep up the ceaseless entertainment factor in their play, the maverick items and choices, and yet still remain rugby's most deadly finishers? It can only be, given the circumstances in which each play, that they are geniuses, nothing less.

It is fatuous to even try to speculate who is the greater, David Campese, Australia's wing, who holds the world record for international tries, or Serge Blanco, the French full-back from Biarritz, who has almost matched him. You can compare the two and say that Blanco's brilliance is more languid with more of the dramatics involved as he gestures upfield from his station, bristling with dark-skinned intent, and savouring the "Blanco ... Blanco ... Blanco" from the crowd at the Parc des Princes.

Those who join the pilgrimage to visit Blanco in his beloved Biarritz, in the south-west corner of France in the Basque country, see a man so laid back as to be almost falling over, a man at peace in the spotlight, who is not con-

ceited, who does not turn the attention and the adoration aside but rather revels in it. When, as a spoof, a French radio station announced that Blanco had gone to Rugby League they had to quickly own up and broadcast a correction; the reaction of the French rugby public was frightening to contemplate.

Campese is less comfortable amongst the acolytes and back slappers; more staccato in his play, more of a jack-in-the-box. Australia does not hold its rugby heroes to its heart as does France but for all that Campese is revered. Like Blanco, his career can flourish without too many career pressures. Campese plays rugby all year round, departing during the southern summer for the northern hemisphere to play in Italy, the land of his family; Blanco puts in three days a week promotional work for a drinks company. They would be the first to admit that this releases them from a grind, allows talent to develop at its own pace, allows fitness to build without the need to fit sessions into crowded lunch hours.

Two glorious entertainers. As a final comparison perhaps you might say, just, that Blanco's brilliance, if a shade more orthodox, accepts principles of back play in rugby carried out at a stratospheric level of greatness, that Campese's brilliance is more off-the-cuff and impossible to predict, that his razor wits permit him to see a space or a possibility three seconds before the players or the cameras or the crowd have realised it is there.

Occasionally, I suppose, Campese's sheer vision for the game, his appetite for the ball and for some buccaneering gesture can lead him towards trouble, as was so glaringly illus-

Blanco (right) rises higher than the rest to gather the ball

80

outstanding Welsh players were attracted North. A. J. Stuart, a former Cardiff player, was an established Dewsbury forward, while another emigrant — also at Dewsbury — was the Wales half-back Bill Stadden.

On the tactical side the debate over the efficiency of the four three-quarter system raged. The Welsh national side, following the Cardiff club example, was committed to the system, but elsewhere, in club and international football, three three-quarters with nine forwards were the norm. Points scoring was not uniform, the outcomes of matches depending on the points systems operated by the Union staging the match. (For instance England's two tries against Scotland were worth two points each according to the SRU system, but two weeks later the tries scored against Ireland were worth only one point each by the RFU system.) The game was played to a rule-book comprising fifty Laws.

OCTOBER
5th . . Newport beat Swansea.

This game, played at Newport, is one of only four defeats for Swansea during the season. But more important, the game marks the senior debut of Billy Bancroft, who is destined to become Wales' most-capped player.

21st . . Yorkshire beat Cumberland.

This is a "friendly" County match, a warm-up game for the Championship matches which begin in November. County football is regarded as the main focus of attention of the game in the North of England, and is well supported.

NOVEMBER
9th . . Yorkshire beat Durham.

Having been declared first County Champions by the RFU in 1889, when Yorkshire were unbeaten in six of their county games, the Yorkshiremen open their Championship defence

Curiously, although the England v Wales match was being played on his home ground, Stadden is the player missing from the Wales team in this photograph taken prior to the game

with a convincing victory against Durham.

16th . . Yorkshire beat Northumberland.

23rd . . Yorkshire beat Lancashire.

The "Roses" match is the third in Yorkshire's County Championship trail and results in a very narrow victory by one goal.

30th . . Richmond beat Blackheath.

This is the first meeting between two of England's oldest and foremost clubs to be held at the Athletic Ground.

Rowland Hill, Secretary of the Rugby Football Union, as seen by Spy in *Vanity Fair*

DECEMBER

9th . . Yorkshire draw with Middlesex.

Despite losing Wise, their Ottley half-back, early in the match, Yorkshire do well to hold Middlesex to a scoreless draw.

14th . . Oxford University beat Cambridge University.

Exceptional interest is generated before the match because the number of wins in the series stands level. Oxford go ahead in the rubber with a decisive win. S. M. J. Woods, the former Australian Test cricketer is the outstanding forward in the Cambridge pack.

16th . . Yorkshire beat Surrey.

21st . . The South beat The North.

The annual match is usually the final trial for the England International side. A. E. Stoddart, the England Test cricketer and Blackheath captain, helps the South to victory with two of his side's four tries at Manchester.

JANUARY 1890

4th . . Yorkshire beat Somerset.

In difficult conditions at Wellington, Yorkshire win by a try to nil. The frosty ground is rendered playable thanks to the magnificent efforts of the Somerset Committee.

6th . . Yorkshire beat Kent.

11th . . Leinster beat Ulster.

The Leinster side, comprising largely Dubliners, beat the Ulstermen for the first time since 1881.

18th . . Leinster beat Munster.

The Leinstermen thus win the Irish Inter-Provincial title outright for the first time since 1877. Six Irish internationals play in the un-beaten side which is tactically controlled from half-back by Lansdowne player, R. G. Warren.

25th . . Blackheath beat Richmond.

Blackheath win their first club match of the decade with traditional rivals Richmond. As the Richmond club enters a period of decline, Blackheath proceed to win every game

Jim Valentine: during the season he scored 61 tries,dropped 5 goals and kicked 35 goals

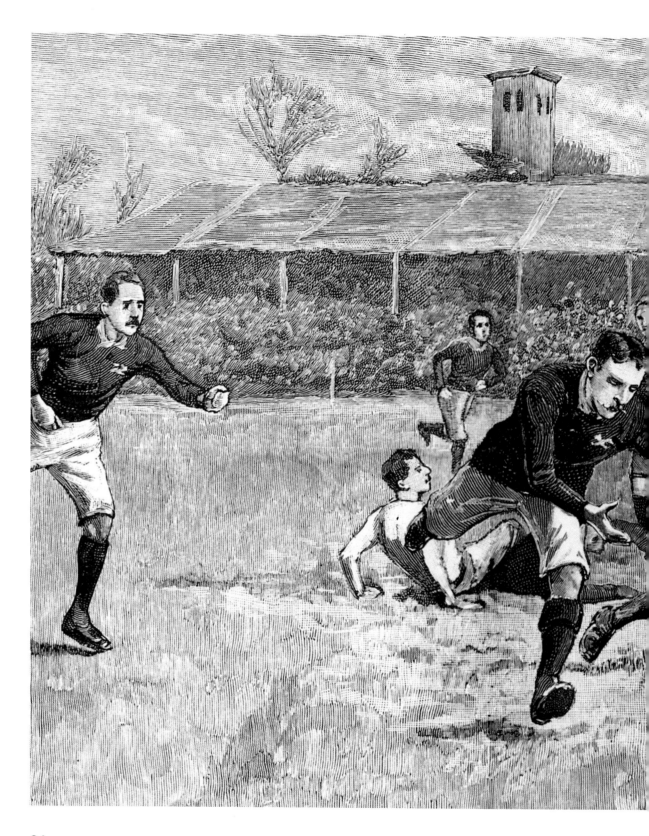

The English
forwards laid the
foundation for the
victory against
Scotland by a goal
and a try to nil

S. M. J. Woods (right), the former Australian Test cricketer, was outstanding for Cambridge in the Varsity Match of 1890, and went on to make his England debut against Wales the following season

Billy Bancroft (far right) made his debut for Wales against Scotland in 1890 and was an ever present in the team, taking every place kick, until 1901

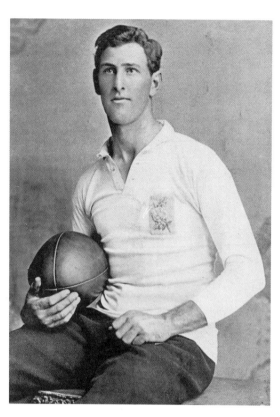

with Richmond during the next half of the decade.

29th . . Blackheath beat Cardiff.

This is only the second ever match between these sides, among the best of their respective countries. In their first visit to the Arms Park, Blackheath field four internationals in their three-quarter line to offset the Cardiff system, and win by a goal to a try in an exciting game.

FEBRUARY

1st . . Scotland beat Wales.

The opening international of the season is notable for the debut in the Welsh side of Billy Bancroft. He enters the Welsh side through the late withdrawal of Newport full-back Tom England, who never again has the opportunity to play for his country.

1st . . The South beat The North.

The second trial of the season, held this time at Richmond, results in another decisive win for the Southerners.

8th . . Yorkshire draw with Cheshire.

After trailing for much of the match, Naylor scores an equalising try for Yorkshire in the closing minutes. Although the conversion from in front of the goal is missed, Yorkshire, by completing an unbeaten season, are declared County Champions.

15th . . Wales beat England.

On a slippery, icy pitch at Dewsbury the Welsh forwards rout the Englishmen to record Wales' first win against England. The only try of the match is scored by Bill Stadden.

22nd . . Scotland beat Ireland.

J. D. Boswell, a rousing forward with a rare penchant for dropping goals from loose play, kicks one of his "specials" to help Scotland to win at Raeburn Place.

22nd . . Yorkshire beat the Rest of England.

The "Challenge" match between the County Champions and the Rest results in a convincing win for Yorkshire at Bradford. The fine play of the home forwards consoles the English selectors, who now turn to five of the successful County pack for the Calcutta Cup match with Scotland.

MARCH

1st . . Ireland and Wales draw.

No St David's Day celebrations for Wales in Dublin. The Welsh are lucky to steal a draw thanks to a late try by Newport's Charlie Thomas, converted by Billy Bancroft.

1st . . England beat Scotland.

In a fine exhibition of rugby the effective teamwork of the English forwards lays the foundation for England's victory.

15th . . England beat Ireland.

A. E. Stoddart captains England to a victory which results in England sharing the International Championship with the Scots. England's success is again attributed to the strength of the Yorkshire forwards forming the nucleus of the side.

The Universities v London and the South at Richmond in 1890

There will be those who will say that the Lions never played any balanced rugby and that they were a side who used only physical aggression to win matches. It is true that they never achieved much in the way of freestyle running, but this was a problem thrust on them by the fanatical obsession of the Australians not to bow the knee by their often questionable alignments in defence. Mark Ella was the only Australian who warmed to the Lions' aggression and remarked: "This is the way we play in the southern hemisphere and unless the Lions face up to it, they are dead."

The tour was marred by the deleterious and wretched attitudes of both sides in the first half of the second Test. This stimulated and provoked a scandalous and venomous concerted campaign against the Lions every day for the whole week before the final Test. The whingeing Pom, it seems, has nothing on the whingeing Australian, as their press, who previously had made little of the tour, suddenly devoted their sports and leader pages to scurrilous attacks on the Lions, particularly on David Young who had stamped on Cutler. No regard was paid to the fact that no one was hurt and while the twenty one year old Young's behaviour was reprehensible and could have seen him taking an early bath, it was far less outrageous than the worst raking of the tour on Mike Hall by Gardner in the Queensland match, which put him off the field, or the dreadful stamping of Gavin Hastings in the NSW game, which left him with a closed and very black eye, or two stampings of Teague.

Matters went from bad to worse when the Australian coach described the Lions as the dirtiest touring team to visit Australia. When I asked him at the press conference at the final test whether he still believed that to be true, his reply was: "that is in my mind."

The Australian Rugby Union poured fuel on the controversy when they issued a

Both David Campese and Gavin Hastings have good reason to remember the third and final test!

Rory Underwood sends the Australian defence the wrong way to set up another attack

statement on the Friday before the climactic last test — the timing was indelicate to say the least. They stated that they condemned violence and that they had directed their Executive Director to prepare a video depicting unacceptable incidents which occurred in the second Test at Ballymore which were believed to be prejudicial to the interests of the game. The video when prepared would be forwarded to the Committee of the Home Unions for their information and for any action which they deemed to be appropriate. In addition the ARFU delegates to the International Board have been asked to raise the matter of video evidence as part of the judicial system.

The four Home Unions and the IRB should have no truck with an edited video and should also demand an explanation from the ARFU regarding the announcement over the public address system, five minutes from the end of the final test, exhorting the crowd to get behind Australia.

In defence of the Lions, I would ask the British Rugby Unions to examine the Lions team and ask themselves in the knowledge of the individuals concerned whether they are type of player to indulge in out and out violence. I am not however suggesting that they were angels, for in the torrid atmosphere of southern hemisphere rugby tensions are bound to be high but what apparently upset the Australians was that the Lions demolished their macho image by the ferocity of their driving and avalanching forward play, which crashed in waves on Australia to break their spirit.

Even after the final test which the Lions won fair and square in a game devoid of any cynical play, apart from an act of petulance by Campese who kicked Sole in the eye after a tackle, the Australian press, to their undying shame, pressed home their attack to the Lions as "scum." The whole matter poses the question that if Test matches adopt the role of wars,

where ferocity turns into thoughtless violence, is the cake worth the eating? And if Australia reacts in this way is it worthwhile the Lions going there in future?

The tour as a whole did not please anybody in the aesthetic sense, an impossibility in the face of the competitive instincts of the Australians, and I repeat that in the second test no one was hurt, apart from stitches as the inevitable result of the force of the forward collision. The malevolence disappeared in the second half when it appeared the referee and the two captains had gained control over the teams.

Off the field the tour had a delightful relaxed ambience. I found the British Lions to be as nice a bunch of men I have toured with. They wholeheartedly embraced a delightful country and the average Australian, who is far different

Aussie captain Nick Farr-Jones, left and opposite page, had a hard time against the Lions

from the image he projects overseas. At home the Australians are forthright, courteous and charming. The Lions did their usual public relations bit by visiting schools and hospitals with unfailing courtesy, they had a lot of fun and did the traditional tourist visit to the Barrier Reef. They went white water rafting, where one boat got into considerable trouble when it overturned and for a couple of minutes there was real

Times correspondent David Hands driving across Sydney Bridge could not understand why the oncoming traffic was weaving from side to side. He was to discover the cause when, a hundred yards further on, he encountered Brian Moore, with his arms out, zooming and banking along the road like an aeroplane. Compassionately Hands picked him up and drove him back to his hangar — such an inci-

concern about David Young, Derek White and Roger Uttley. They held their players courts with their customary outrageous charges. Devereux was charged with lowering the intelligence of the party, Guscott for confusing them by being neither black nor white, and Chris Oti for embarrassing the rest in the showers. All good clean fun.

They always conducted themselves well in terms of dress and behaviour and it was a tour devoid of scandal. They had a few beers and enjoyed themselves but essentially they never drank to excess, apart perhaps from the night of the winning of the series in Sydney. The

dent is part of the legend of such tours and on such a night Brian could be forgiven.

It was the first ever short tour by the Lions comprising only twelve matches, which gave them six matches to identify their Test team before the first Test in Sydney. Clive Rowlands thought this was time enough, for as he pointed out: "We ought to know most of our test side before we left home." He believes however that any future tour should be two weeks longer to give more time for preparation and recovery from injury between the three Tests which on this tour were played on consecutive Saturdays.

2.30 pm: A ball boy presents the match ball to the referee, Irishman Stephen Hilditch who had been in charge of the England v Wales encounter here last year. The tension mounts in the dressing room and to make sure the players are on time all the clocks are set three minutes fast in another of Twickenham's quirky traditions. The reserves, in their thermal tracksuits, are taken into the stands and, with a roar, the players emerge onto Twickenham's famous turf. The dressing rooms are locked as the national anthems play and Ken Cox and John Clark remove the strip of coconut matting used by the visiting dignitaries when meeting the teams.

2.45 pm: The bars, dining areas and car parks fall silent as the game kicks off and 62,500 pairs of eyes attempt to focus on 30 men chasing the Gilbert Barabarian around the Rugby Union's most famous patch of turf.

3.10 pm: As England's captain Will Carling slices through the French defence to score the opening try, the dressing room area sees its first casualty. So unremitting are the clashes between the packs that Claude Portolan, the 18-stone French tighthead prop, has come off the field with damaged ribs. He is replaced by Jean-Pierre Garuet.

4.05 pm: Up in the BBC radio commentary box Pierre Villepreux, the coach of Toulouse and one-time France full-back, is adding a touch of spice to the occasion by giving his comments on the game to an English audience. A rival of the French coach Jacques Fouroux, Villepreux has helped to coach England this season. On the pitch his coaching seems to have worked as Andy Robinson, the English openside flanker, administers *le dernier coup* with a second try in the final minute. England win 11 - 0, their first victory over France in seven years.

4.15 pm: As the players troop off the pitch and back into their dressing rooms they are handed shandies from a cupboard. Some choose to luxuriate in the famous cast-iron baths which have been here since 1931, others stand under the showers.

4.30 pm: The post-match inquest begins. The BBC have a small corner in the dressing room area and a triumphant Will Carling gives his opinion of his try: "It was probably the worst move we've done all season."

5 pm: A press room next to the dressing room is a new innovation at Twickenham. From here a video camera can send pictures back to the main press room in the east stand opposite. Geoff Cooke, the England manager, and Roger Uttley, the England coach, are suitably chuffed. Jacques Fouroux, a natty lilac silk handkerchief in the top pocket of his dark blue blazer, is generous in his praise of England and he calls his own side "heroic" for keeping the score to respectable proportions. But to French journalists he is bitter at "les insultes" and "les grimaces" of the English forwards. The newspaper men have their stories. Villepreux gives his own press conference: "Maybe now England will do even better if I teach them how to link the forwards to the backs, yes?" he jokes.

5.15 pm: The bars are already closing and the fans melt away. Police say that the crowds have been well behaved and they have arrested a streaker. Among the soft rosewood panelling and velvet drapes of the Rose Room the players, battered, bruised and after-shaved, mingle with their families. Later the teams will meet again at the after-match banquet.

6.30 pm: The stand and concourse lighting that has been on since the end of the game is switched off and the gates are locked.

8 pm: The car park gates close but they are opened again on the Sunday morning between 10 am and midday when some of those well stocked Volvos are collected by bleary-eyed owners. Twenty cleaners arrive the next day and John Clark and his staff are already preparing for next Saturday and the Army v Royal Navy match.

Just for fun?...
the role of sevens

Nick Cain

Bristol meet Blackheath at the Middlesex Sevens in 1989

"Sevens should be fun, it's just an end of season jaunt and it shouldn't be taken too seriously."

The words of an esteemed colleague bounced off the walls of the Press Room at Twickenham. In a nutshell he had presented the "establishment" view of the abbreviated code, and what more appropriate venue to do so than the Middlesex Sevens. The strange thing was that he then proceeded to landmine his own

argument by lamenting the falling standards of sevens expertise on show at this great event. "There's only one side out there today that knows how to play and that's the Quins... and they wouldn't have stood a chance against those Loughborough Colleges and London Welsh sides of the seventies."

Agreed, the standard fare on on show would have seen most of the participants relegated to the Plate or Bowl competitions at the

Hong Kong Sevens, the world's premier sevens event, but you can expect little more if you cast sevens in the role of being "just a bit of fun." Sure it's fun, in the same way as fifteen a side is fun. Rugby is meant to be fun, isn't it? But there are other factors too: the satisfying of the competitive instinct in a physical contact game of pace and guile that demands the highest standards of fitness, these are as much in demand in the abbreviated game as in the full version.

The "sevens for fun" argument can be taken too far. Try telling that to Rosslyn Park who had just gone through a lung-bursting afternoon of frenetic endeavour to fall at the final hurdle to the Quins! Anybody who has played the shortened code knows you would get short shrift: sevens is as demanding as fifteens, moreso in purely respiratory terms, and far more cruel at exposing any weaknesses in individual players. According to All Black captain David Kirk: "Sevens exposes the flaws in one's game. You can't hide your inability to pass, to take a pass, deliver and catch. Sevens is merciless."

Kirk has a good vantage point as he was a participant in a revolution in New Zealand thinking towards the abbreviated game which has subsequently banished the "establishment" view to the sidelines down under. The Hong Kong Sevens has provided the New Zealanders

Brunei take on Singapore at the Cathay Pacific Hong Kong sevens

Putt of New Zealand breaks clear in the 1989 Cathay Pacific Hong Kong sevens final against Australia

with the opportunity to take stock of sevens, and it did not take them long to discover that it could provide them with an invaluable testing ground for talented up-and-comers. One of the secrets behind the pre-eminence of New Zealand rugby is that they organise more efficiently than their rivals and Hong Kong provided them with the sort of gift-horse that they could never look in the mouth. During the late seventies the Kiwis dabbled with the event and sent provincial sides like Manawatu, Auckland and Marlborough to contest the issue and, up until 1986, they had registered just one win when the Cantabrians, an invitation side, were successful in the inaugural event a decade earlier.

The New Zealanders started fielding their national seven in 1983 and it wasn't all roses as the following year the Fijians hammered them 26 - 0 in the final. But the die was cast. A year later coach Bryce Rope told me with disarming candour, "We don't play sevens very much in New Zealand, if at all." He then proceeded to explain to me how a domestic sevens competition had been introduced three years earlier involving all 26 provinces.

The following year (1986) Rope arrived in Hong Kong with a world-beating outfit, including Kirk and yet-to-be All Blacks Wayne Shelford, Zinzan Brooke, Frano Botica and Mark Brooke-Cowden, which blasted aside all opposition from the Crown Colony to Cardiff (the Sport Aid Sevens) with an unstoppable brand of power-play sevens. They have made the final in Hong Kong every year since then, winning in '87, losing to the Wallabies by the narrowest of margins in '88, and brushing them aside in '89 to gain revenge.

And while only a fool would suggest that sevens provides a good yardstick with which to measure the front five forwards, only a fool would deny that it provides exactly that for the backs and back row forwards. The New Zealanders have used sevens to the All Blacks

benefit in no uncertain terms. Yesterday's Shelford, Brooke or Botica is today's Seymour, Rush or Putt — three names to watch out for on the evidence of this year's Hong Kong action. But while the Kiwis make the most of Hong Kong the RFU, alongside the other British unions, have steadfastly refused to send national sides to the event. Meanwhile the standard at the Middlesex Sevens continues to fall...

Thankfully it still commands sufficient attention to provide a platform for talented young performers like Harlequins flanker Chris Sheasby to make their mark. But today's sell-out crowds could be tomorrow's empty seats

unless the Middlesex tournament gets to grips with the changing face of sevens and revamps itself. Why not make room for an overseas invitation side each year — such as the Fijians — to come and play with the boys. The players would love it, the crowd would love it, and it wouldn't spoil the fun or break the bank.

Let's give our players the platform by restoring sevens to the status it deserves, otherwise English rugby will ultimately be the loser.

Moseley and Sale in a tangle during the inaugural Wang Sevens tournament

The history of the Varsity Match

David Lawrenson

It is hard to think of many sporting events which would attract 50,000 spectators to watch two teams of students battle it out on a Tuesday afternoon in December but such is the standing and tradition of the Oxford v Cambridge Varsity Match that it has become, along with the Boat Race, the Grand National and Wimbledon, one of the major events on the British sporting calendar. In these days of corporate hospitality and sponsorship, it is perhaps not hard to see why the Varsity Match, which is dominated by high flyers both on and off the pitch, has attained the status it has, but it wasn't always so.

The fixture has had a chequered history, in fact during the late Sixties and early Seventies it was in real danger of dying as crowds shrank to just over 20,000 and the games were desperately dull. But a look into the history of the event reveals the real secret of its success over the century. The Varsity Match has played host to some of the greatest players ever to grace the sport, who have come from all parts of the globe to do battle in blue. Perhaps most importantly, for much of the history of the game Oxford and Cambridge were in the vanguard of innovation. Their training methods, tactics etc. were light years ahead of anything elsewhere, and indeed things learned at Grange Road and Iffley Road were often taken back to clubs both in Britain and abroad. Oxbridge rugby influence really did span continents and help in the development of the world game.

The beginnings of the great occasion were suitably inauspicious. The first game was

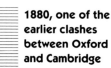
1880, one of the earlier clashes between Oxford and Cambridge

held on February 10th, 1872 in the Parks at Oxford and was the result of a discussion between H. A. Hamilton of Cambridge and an Oxford counterpart C. W. L. Bulpett. Rugby as a sport was still in its infancy with the Rugby Football Union having only been founded a year earlier. Oxford had been quick off the mark, forming a club in 1869 with Cambridge following suit three years later. Rugby had been evolving steadily during the early part of the century, but even in that first Varsity Match they played with 20 on each side.

The first fixture had a few teething problems, not least being the unavailability of the Cambridge captain E. Winnington-Ingram. He was forced to pull out because of his studies so the team made the awkward cross country train journey to Oxford led by I. C. Lambert. While Oxford took the field in their famous dark blue, Cambridge wore pink for the occa-

sion, but luckily they soon adopted a more appropriate light blue. Even in that first game the teams were experimenting with tactics, Cambridge opting to play 15 forwards while Oxford relied on 14 with the extra man in the backs. It paid off because the Dark Blues won that first encounter by one goal to nil.

.G.OWEN-SMITH (B) ✳ V.G.J.JENKINS (¾) H.D.B.LORRAINE(¾) ✳ P.C.MINNS(¾) S.L.WAIDE(¾)

K.L.T.JACKSON(½) ✳ N.K.LAMPORT(½) C.A.L.RICHARDS(F) ✳ E.S.NICHOLSON(F) M.F.PEACOCK(F)

.E.S.CHARLES(F) ✳ K.W.J.JONES(F) R.E.PRESCOTT(F) J.B.BOWERS(F) H.M.KELLY(F)

The Oxford XV of 1932 who beat Cambridge by eight points to three to take a 26 to 21 lead in the series of matches

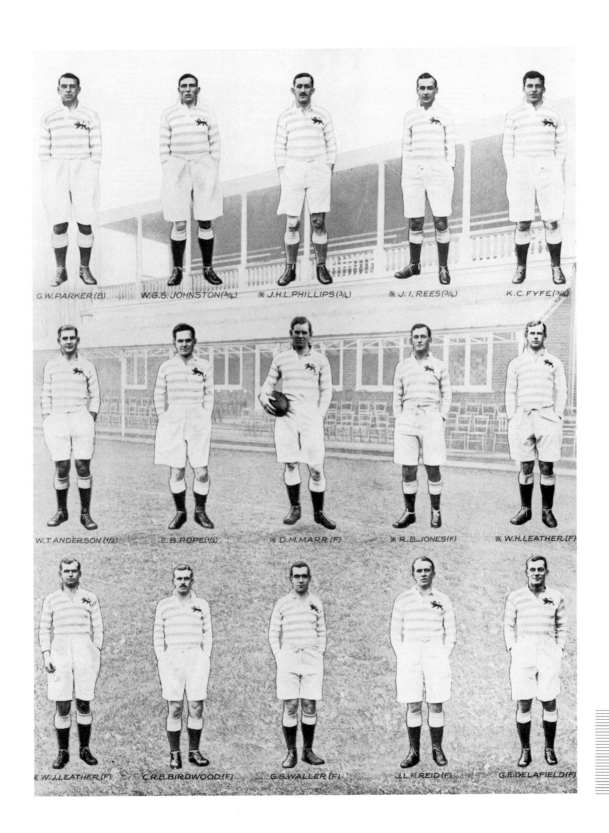

G.W. PARKER (B)   W.G.S. JOHNSTON (3/4)   ※ J.H.L. PHILLIPS (3/4)   ※ J.I. REES (3/4)   K.C. FYFE (3/4)

W.T. ANDERSON (1/2)   E.B. POPE (1/2)   ※ D.M. MARR (F)   ※ R.B. JONES (F)   ※ W.H. LEATHER (F)

※ W.J. LEATHER (F)   C.R.B. BIRDWOOD (F)   G.S. WALLER (F)   J.L.P. REID (F)   G.E. DELAFIELD (F)

The Cambridge XV
of 1932 pictured, as
are the Oxford XV
opposite, with their
home pavilion in
the background

Action from the Varsity Match in 1900 played at Queen's Club, Kensington

Although the next year's return match was held at Cambridge, it was decided that subsequent matches should be played on neutral ground in London. Over the years the Oval, Blackheath and the Queen's Club in Kensington played host to the students before the fixture was eventually moved to Twickenham in 1921. By this time the teams were down to 15 a side and playing under laws which we would recognise today. The Oxbridge brand of rugby became popular and in 1911 the match attracted a crowd of 16,000. It was the continued success of the fixture which prompted the move to Twickenham. By 1923 the attendance had reached 30,000 and a couple of years later touched 40,000.

During this time Cambridge came under the influence of Wavell (later Lord) Wakefield, one of the legendary figures of the game. He was already the leader of the England pack by the time he arrived at the university and made an indelible mark on Cambrige rugby while he was there. He invited great players down to give their opinions on the team and the players, some 40 years before most club sides would ever dream of having a coach, and was a master of tactics.

The fitness levels and tactical appreciation of the two university sides put them streets ahead of the club sides and not surprisingly the Varsity Match was seen very much as a traditional trial for the England team. But both teams, particularly Oxford through the Rhodes Scholarship scheme, benefited from numerous talented players who weren't home grown. In 1931 there wasn't an Englishman in the Oxford back line, the full back was Welsh, one wing was a New Zealander and the other an American, the centres were Welsh and South African, the fly-half was Welsh and the scrum-half Australian.

Probably the most dashing figure ever to grace a Varsity match came from the most unusual background of all. Alexander Obolensky was a Russian Prince, the son of an officer in the Tsar's Imperial Horse Guard. He was brought to England as a baby to escape the Russian Revolution and ended up at Trent College. He made a name for himself as a sprinter but he could also play rugby. He went up to Oxford and won his first blue in 1935. Most of us tend to think that lightweight boots are a modern development but Obolensky was keen to reproduce his speed of the track on the rugby field. He became a regular visitor to Elmer Cotton's sports shop in the Turl searching for lighter and thinner boots and often they were so delicately made that they wouldn't even last out one match. A flamboyant character, Obolensky is said to have developed the habit of consuming a dozen oysters before taking the field for any match he played in the London area.

He played in the 1935 and 1937 Varsity Matches, missing out on one because of a hamstring injury. In 1936 he played for England against the touring All Blacks and scored one of the finest tries ever seen at Twickenham. Although he never scored in his two Varsity Match appearances Obolensky saved the 1935 game for Oxford by racing across to the opposite side of the field and tackling the Cambridge wing Rawlence into touch a foot from the try line. Sadly the Russian Prince became the first rugby international to lose his life in the Second World War when the fighter he was piloting on a training flight crashed in 1940.

Crowds of over 30,000 were commonplace for the fixture and after the war they climbed even higher. 1949 saw the biggest ever crowd and probably the most famous incident in the history of the fixture. 59,400 turned up to watch a host of star names but the game was chiefly remembered for a spectacular clash between two future presidents of the RFU, J. V. Smith and John Kendall-Carpenter.

John Kendall-Carpenter, now chairman of the IRFB, saved the game in spectacular fashion for Oxford in 1949

"I thought my only chance was to go hard at him and hope that the momentum would carry me over the line with the tackle. But his weight and speed and the angle he was coming at meant he tackled me into touch about five yards short." Oxford hung on to win the game but Smith remains bemused as to why a prop should have been in that position on the field anyway. Kendall-Carpenter maintains that it was training as a no. 8 which saved the day. Because Hofmeyr hadn't found touch with his kick, Kendall-Carpenter instinctively set off across the field to cover, as a no. 8 used to in those days.

"Although I was playing prop that day I was still a no. 8 by instinct so I stayed back. The interesting thing was that JV couldn't quite come inside me and ought to have gone outside, but he hesitated and I think our eyes met. I saw a hunted look and I knew then that he was my captive and I eventually tackled him into touch."

1959 saw one of the more unusual sights in Varsity Match rugby. Oxford fielded a big wing three-quarter from the USA named Pete Dawkins who had never played rugby before he arrived in England. But he was a superb all round athlete and an A1 American footballer, and soon adapted. Like Fredie Hovde 30 years earlier, Oxford used him to throw in at the line-outs like a Gridiron quarter back and in fact two of his torpedoes went straight to his captain Malcom Phillips in the centre.

In the Sixties the Varsity Match played host to a crop of great players including Irishman Mike Gibson, who played in three and captained Cambridge in 1965. But things began to slide, the powers-that-be seemed more interested in academic qualifications than any sporting talents and the general public's interest in the fixture began to wane. 1967 was generally agreed to be the dullest Varsity Match ever, in fact so poor was the game that the Cambridge skipper, Martin Green, went into print in the

Kendall-Carpenter was a fast, open-side wing forward but such was the wealth of talent at Oxford at the time, particularly from overseas, that he entered the 1949 match as a tight head prop. Smith, who was small and quick, went on to win all his England caps on the wing but on that day played in the centre for Cambridge. The game proved pretty uninspiring and Oxford had a 3 - 0 lead with just minutes to go. Their full back Hofmeyr kicked the ball deep into Cambridge territory but hadn't found touch and a loose scrum developed. Cambridge eventually worked the ball back to Smith who was waiting on the blindside touchline and the little centre was off. He raced up the touchline beat the immediate cover and then swerved outside the full back. He was now 40 yards out and bearing down on the line when out of the corner of his eye he saw Kendall-Carpenter running at a right angle to head him off before the line. Smith thought about cutting inside but knew the cover would get him if he did.

Halliday in action scoring against Wasps

if they want to return for the opening matches in the Courage Championship to get themselves in shape for England's game against Fiji in November. Of course the exposure to different syles of play, to different, perhaps more rigorous attitudes, would be of great benefit; of course the opportunity for travel and making new friends, which I still believe to be a prime aim of rugby, would be tremendous, but how do you get a rest from such a schedule ?" The answer is undoubtedly a change in attitudes at selection. Rather than insisting that the best 15 players are selected for every 1st XV fixture, clubs will have to broaden their base of players.

Last year for example Bath used 49 players in the 1st XV. In short, some games would become more important than others. Players would soon become used to the idea, as would spectators. The second-string games would serve a useful purpose in grooming players for the future. If the programme were to become more streamlined with perhaps only 20 top grade games it may even help players with quality of performance becoming more important than quantity of games played.

Of course none of this can be achieved without money. There is little doubt that only a handful of clubs would have the resources in terms of manpower, crowds and sponsorship potential, to generate the finance. Bath, Leicester, Gloucester and possibly a Midland or London club might make up the English representation. Will top players then gravitate towards these clubs? Almost inevitably, which would be a good thing for the game at international level. Some will question whether such a trend would be good for the game as a whole, muttering darkly about elitism, disappearance of club loyalty, increased pressures and so on. It could still be a good thing for the game at every level if people were to recognise that rugby union is no longer one game but is now two. 99% of players play the game for fun — a bit of exercise and a few beers, occasionally both at the same time. Domestic rugby for them will not change one jot in the next five or fifty years. The remaining 1% of the rugby playing population play the game for added reasons, still for fun, beer and exercise, but also for personal fulfilment and an obligation or an urge to express the supreme gifts that God or someone has given them. There is no reason why these two tiers of the game cannot happily co-exist.

If such a scenario were to come to pass there would inevitably be a call at some point for some sort of reimbursement for players at the top level. Already there would seem to be significant support from the southern hemisphere for a trust fund system to be established. Other amateur sports have embraced such a notion and survived. Rugby, being a team sport, is in more of a quandary. Who gets what ? Will an unglamorous prop forward get cheesed off when the prima donna high earner at fly-half misses six kicks at goal? It is a complex problem

and one which will require great sensitivity, understanding and perception to solve. Quite what will evolve in the next five to ten years is difficult to predict but there is already evidence of a burgeoning European dimension in the club scene.

COACHING AND ADMINISTRATION

The backbone of every club is the volunteer. The bar-manager, pie n' beans cook, the treasurer, the social secretary, the fund raiser, the car park official, the programme editor... the list is endless. There will always be a place in rugby clubs for such people but many senior clubs are now facing up to the enormous demands being made on the principal administrators. Some, like Northampton, have already recognised the need for a full-time professional administrator. It's likely that within the next ten years all the senior clubs will employ someone in such a capacity. Clubs will have to be run on much more business-like lines if they are to survive. As with the administrators so too perhaps with coaches. The roles in fact may overlap. In the close season Norwich of London Division 2 North, and ambitious for a higher level of rugby, advertised for a "Coaching/Playing Administrator" offering a salary in the region of £15-20,000.

Although "technical administrators" have existed at Twickenham for almost 20 years, the RFU are very wary of this new trend. They sent a circular to all clubs pointing out that any club intending to appoint such a person should first supply the secretary of the RFU with a copy of the job description. This was designed to safeguard the amateur regulations which prevent a salaried official from coaching a specific team or acting as a selector.

There is no doubt that such quibbling with semantics will, or at least should, become an irrelevance in the next ten years. Tom Hudson at Bath points to other amateur sports as an example of professional coaches coexisting with unpaid performers. "Swimming, boxing, rowing have all taken such a step forward," he says. "Indeed the national association of coaches sees it as desirable that performers should have such expert, specialist advice available to them. If the players are putting more and more time into the game it is only fair that they should get the best. It takes far longer to plan a session than to actually do it."

His view is supported by Geoff Cooke who as well as being the England manager is also the chief executive of the British Association of National Coaches.

"Professional coaches in rugby union is an inevitable and desirable development," he says. "I have no difficulty in reconciling that point of view with players not being paid. A coach may be involved far longer in the sport, he has a level expertise accrued over a number of years, a player has much different motivations and so on. The bedrock of the sport will not change too much because most clubs will not be able to support a paid official, be he an administrator or a coach."

Cooke also envisages the day, probably within the next 10 years, when the post of England manager is a full-time paid job. Only that way can the proper amount of time be given over to the full and considered preparation of the international team. It may be that some arrangement will have to be struck between the RFU and employers, perhaps seconding the person from their job for a 4-year period.

At the sharp end coaching itself will also undergo change in the next decade. More and more senior clubs as well as the national team will use sports science to supplement their training programmes. England has successfully assimilated some of the up-to-date work into physical preparation in a bid to boost their fitness levels. Bath too have successfully

England manager Geoff Cooke feels that the advent of the professional rugby coach is inevitable

incorporated physiological testing into their programme. It is the pyschological preparation of players which needs an enormous amount of work and is an area which will come to the fore. The mental peaking of a player cannot be divorced from his physical preparation but at the moment for example it would seem that England, with all their resources, are under-achieving. As the Americans and East Germans have proved, psychological tuning is vital to success. We will also see an enormous development in technology as a coaching aid, be it video, computer graphics or machines to monitor physiological progress.

THE MEDIA

Rugby has never been more popular. At least among the media it hasn't. All newspapers now devote far more column inches to the sport than ever and with the advent of leagues even thetabloids have got in on the act. The World Cup in 1991 is certain to generate enormous interest, particularly if there are some vibrant performances from the home nations. The catalyst for this increased interest has not just been the sport itself — full of drama and athleticism as it is — but also the involvement of sponsors. If Courage, Pilkington, Save and Prosper or whoever put a fair amount of money into the game, then they quite rightly expect some sort of return from that investment. They therefore commission a public relations company to ensure that they get as much publicity via the media as possible. It's a scenario which is likely to increase enormously in the next ten years. It will mean that at all levels of the game clubs, if they are to fulfil their obligations to sponsors, will have to gear themselves up to the needs of the media, i.e. better press and television facilities, easier access to players and officials, and improved communications all round.

Money and sport is not an easy partnership however. It needs sensitive, sure handling. Money must never dominate the sport and similarly sport should not take a sponsor's money on false pretences. The money accrued through sponsorship is, and will increasingly be, of enormous benefit to the game. The real core of this relationship is television. Television opens the door to a potential wealth of riches — not just ground advertising, particularly now that revolving advertising boards are coming more into use.

The real money to be made is in having control of the whole operation. If the Home Unions were to control proceedings themselves then their return could increase enormously, as it is they have not got any direct broadcasting or satellite facilities and are not able to originate the signals for broadcasting themselves. They rely on the companies to import their own temporary studios. If the Unions could install their own facilities and camera points they could then source the pictures themselves and consequently sell the access for a much higher return.

The actual presentation of the sport, i.e. whatever the viewer sees on the screen, is dictated by the amount of money put into the production. With a higher profile and increasing investment the packaging of the sport can, one hopes, only get better.

INTERNATIONAL

In the next decade the World Cup will become the fulcrum of an international team's programme. The importance of winning the competition, be it merely to satisfy personal and national pride or the need to stimulate the game within the country, will be acknowledged more and more. Already England are planning in four year cycles and as Geoff Cooke points out, they are already thinking of the World Cup in 1995 as well.

"Our aim in the build up to a World Cup will be to expose as many players as possible to the conditions likely to prevail in that country. The existence of the World Cup will also affect the type of international opposition we are likely to play outside the mainstream of the Five Nations. For example, we may wish to groom players in which case we may try to play one of the lesser countries, or arrange a B fixture or look to play at senior and U-21 levels."

The structure of the season will continue to be an area of fierce debate, particularly the role of the divisions and the counties. Cooke for example is very much in favour of the divisions as the stepping stone to international level whilst others see the concentration of talent in half a dozen top clubs as the way forward.

As for playing developments... Russia to beat an IB country by 1999? America to win the World Cup within 20 years? England to beat Wales in Cardiff? Jacques Fouroux to select Serge Blanco at hooker? Will Carling to be appointed captain for the 21st century?

Statistics

COURAGE CLUBS CHAMPIONSHIP 1988-89

National Division 1

Club	Pld	Won	Drn	Lost	For	Agn	Pts
Bath	11	10	0	1	263	98	20
Gloucester	11	7	1	3	215	112	15
Wasps	11	7	1	3	206	138	15
Nottingham	11	6	1	4	142	122	13
Orrell	11	6	1	4	148	157	13
Leicester	11	6	1	4	189	199	13
Bristol	11	6	0	5	188	117	12
Harlequins	11	5	0	6	194	184	10
Rosslyn Park	11	5	0	6	172	208	10
Moseley	11	3	0	8	113	242	6
Waterloo	11	1	1	9	120	235	3
L'pool St Helens	11	1	0	10	116	254	2

Bath win the championship, Waterloo and Liverpool St Helens are relegated to the second division

National Division 2

Club	Pld	Won	Drn	Lost	For	Agn	Pts
Saracens	11	11	0	0	288	80	22
Bedford	11	6	2	3	141	187	14
Northampton	11	6	1	4	165	131	13
Sale	11	5	2	4	195	152	12
Coventry	11	6	0	5	150	143	12
London Irish	11	5	2	4	194	222	12
Headingley	11	5	1	5	179	136	11
Blackheath	11	4	1	6	181	144	9
Richmond	11	4	1	6	112	216	9
Gosforth	11	4	0	7	176	246	8
London Scottish	11	3	1	7	146	160	7
London Welsh	11	1	1	9	125	235	3

Saracens and Bedford are promoted to the first division, London Scottish and London Welsh are relegated to the third division

National Division 3

Club	Pld	Won	Drn	Lost	For	Agn	Pts
Plymouth Albion	11	11	0	0	311	89	22
Rugby	11	10	0	1	268	99	20
Wakefield	11	9	0	2	282	114	18
West Hartlepool	11	5	1	5	164	133	11
Nuneaton	11	5	0	6	178	214	10
Sheffield	11	4	1	6	170	182	9
Vale of Lune	11	4	1	6	120	145	9
Askeans	11	4	1	6	141	215	9
Exeter	11	4	0	7	142	180	8
Fylde	11	4	0	7	136	181	8
Met Police	11	4	0	7	130	275	8
Maidstone	11	0	0	11	74	289	0

Plymouth Albion and Rugby are promoted to the second division, Metropolitan Police and Maidstone are relegated to the area leagues

Area League North

Club	Pld	Won	Drn	Lost	For	Agn	Pts
Roundhay	10	8	1	1	235	81	17
Broughton Park	10	8	0	2	179	92	16
Stourbridge	10	6	0	4	118	79	12
Northern	10	5	0	5	182	131	10
Winnington Park	10	5	0	5	188	155	10
Preston G'ppers	10	5	0	5	161	141	10
Durham City	10	5	0	5	172	157	10
Morley	10	5	0	5	135	141	10
Lichfield	10	4	1	5	112	113	9
Stoke on Trent	10	3	0	7	88	138	6
Birmingham	10	0	0	10	29	371	0

Roundhay are promoted to National Division 3, Birmingham are relegated

Area League South

Club	Pld	Won	Drn	Lost	For	Agn	Pts
Lydney	10	8	1	1	240	98	17
Havant	10	8	1	1	177	92	17
Camborne	10	6	1	3	198	126	13
Redruth	10	6	1	3	136	81	13
Sudbury	10	5	1	4	141	89	11
Cheltenham	10	4	2	4	122	151	10
Salisbury	10	4	1	5	113	139	9
Southend	10	4	0	6	116	168	8
Ealing	10	3	0	7	144	188	6
Stroud	10	3	0	7	119	180	6
Sidcup	10	0	0	10	74	268	0

Lydney are promoted to National Division 3, Ealing, Stroud and Sidcup are relegated

Pilkington Cup 1988-89 results

ROUND 1 Saturday 17th September 1988

Guildf'd & G'ming	12	v 20	Old Culverhasians
Medway	11	v 9	Old Mid Whitgiftians
Berry Hill	18	v 7	Askeans
Brixham	38	v 9	Okehampton
Swindon	22	v 0	Ruislip
North Walsham	38	v 6	Old Judians
Combe Down	19	v 24	Havant
Oxford	17	v 6	Tabard
Finchley	10	v 9	Lydney
Marlow	15	v 37	Maidstone
Metropolitan Police	13	v 11	Reading
Exeter	40	v 12	Sudbury
Barking	12	v 7	Ealing
Redruth	21	v 6	Worthing
Sandal	0	v 3	Durham City
Rugby	27	v 6	Vale of Lune
Newark	6	v 12	Winnington Park
Birkenhead Park	13	v 7	Bedworth
Middlesbrough	30	v 21	West Park
Harrogate	10	v 22	West Hartlepool
Widnes	16	v 13	Bromsgrove
Stoneygate	9	v 30	Nuneaton
Matlock	12	v 34	Aspatria
Plymouth Albion	60	v 3	Stoke Old Boys
Sheffield	3	v 16	Wakefield
Hereford	18	v 12	Leighton Buzzard
Tynedale	15	v 0	Stockwood Park
Fylde	17	v 6	Wolverhampton

ROUND 2 Saturday 5th November 1988

Winnington Park	4	v 37	Northampton
Durham City	19	v 10	Sale
Coventry	7	v 12	Plymouth Albion
Hereford	28	v 9	Widnes
Middlesbrough	12	v 18	Aspatria
Birkenhead Park	3	v 38	Tynedale
Gosforth	31	v 10	Fylde
Headingley	7	v 10	Wakefield
West Hartlepool	9	v 30	Rugby
Bedford	16	v 0	Nuneaton
North Walsham	3	v 31	Saracens
Maidstone	12	v 37	London Scottish
Exeter	18	v 3	Redruth
Berry Hill	24	v 9	London Welsh
Swindon	3	v 13	Blackheath
Old Culverhasians	3	v 13	Brixham
London Irish	25	v 13	Metropolitan Police
Medway	9	v 30	Havant
Oxford	28	v 0	Barking
Finchley	6	v 40	Richmond

ROUND 3 Saturday 28th January 1989

Brixham	4	v 28	Gloucester
Gosforth	9	v 29	Wakefield
Wasps	33	v 3	Durham City
Bedford	3	v 6	Nottingham
Bath	82	v 9	Oxford
Blackheath	6	v 13	Waterloo
Rugby	3	v 25	Harlequins
London Scottish	16	v 0	Saracens
Havant	9	v 3	Exeter
Bristol	13	v 7	Orrell
Rosslyn Park	18	v 0	Plymouth Albion
London Irish	14	v 3	Berry Hill
Hereford	10	v 6	Tynedale
Liverpool	6	v 37	Leicester
Aspatria	6	v 3	Moseley
Richmond	6	v 0	Northampton

ROUND 4 Saturday 11th February 1989

Wasps	39	v 7	Aspatria
Bath	48	v 0	Hereford
Harlequins	22	v 6	London Scottish
Bristol	45	v 16	London Irish
Gloucester	19	v 16	Waterloo
Wakefield	18	v 10	Havant
Richmond	9	v 12	Nottingham
Rosslyn Park	9	v 23	Leicester

QUARTER FINALS Saturday 25th February 1989

Harlequins	15	v 9	Nottingham
Bath	14	v 12	Bristol
Leicester	22	v 18	Wasps
Wakefield	13	v 28	Gloucester

SEMI-FINALS Saturday 25th March 1989

Gloucester	3	v 6	Bath
Harlequins	7	v 16	Leicester

FINAL Saturday 29th April 1989

Leicester	6	v 10	Bath

Statistics on the 1988 Bicentennial Wallaby trip to England, Scotland and Italy

15 matches: 11 wins, four losses; 438 points for, 236 against.

Total tries: 68 for, 29 against (or 4.8 per match).

Leading try scorers: David Campese 15, James Grant 8,

Acura Niuqila 6, David Knox 5.

Leading points scorers: Michael Lynagh 80, David Campese 72,

David Knox 69.

New caps: Brad Girvan (England), Brad Burke, Scott Gourley,

Acura Niuqila (Scotland) .

Scores

London Division 21 bt Australia 10 (Oct 15)

Northern Division 15 bt Australia 9 (Oct 19)

Australia 37 bt England B 9 (Oct 22)

South West Div 26 bt Australia 10 (Oct 26)

Australia 25 bt Midland Div 18 (Oct 29)

Australia 56 bt Combined Students (Nov 1)

England 28 bt Australia 19 (Nov 5)

Australia 25 bt Edinburgh 19 (Nov 9)

Australia 29 bt South of Scotland 4 (Nov 12)

Australia 37 bt North and Midlands 17 (Nov 15)

Australia 32 bt Scotland 13 (Nov 19)

Australia 48 bt Combined Services 7 (Nov 22)

Australia 40 bt Barbarians 22 (Nov 26)

Australia 26 bt Italy B 18 (Nov 30)

Australia 55 bt Italy 6 (Dec 3)

Tries by David Campese and Serge Blanco (to April 30th 1989)

Scored against	Campese	Blanco
France	2	-
Australia	–	3
England	3	1
Scotland	4	5
Ireland	0	4
Wales	0	4
New Zealand	5	1
Argentina	4	6
• Other	14	3
Total	32	27

Dusty Hare Career Statistics

Points totals

Nottingham	1800
Leicester	4507
England	240
British Lions	88
Others	598
Total	**7118**

Records

England
Most points: 240
Most points in a season: 44 (1983-84)
Most penalties: 67

Leicester
Most points in a season: 438 (1988-89)

Index

Picture acknowledgements
The publishers wish to thank the following sources for their help in providing illustrations.

Allsport Photographic 37, 38, 70, 83. Simon Bruty 12, 13, 41, 42, 44, 46, 73, 125, 131. David Cannon 69. Russell Cheyne 8, 9, 10, 15, 16, 17, 18, 20, 21, 22, 24, 26, 29, 31, 32, 47, 49, 51, 64, 65, 66, 68, 72, 75, 76-77, 78, 79, 81, 82, 88, 101, 103, 104, 106 (below), 109 (below), 110-111, 112, 115 (below), 116, 117, 120, 122, 128, 129,130, 138, 140, 142, 143, 144, 145, 146, 148, 149, 151. Andrew Gatt 23. Roger Labrosse 36. Bob Martin 33, 45, 126. Ben Radford 19, 39, 71, 119. Chris Raphael 90. Pascal Rondeau 141. Dan Smith 34, 35.
Allsport USA Mike Powell 27, 40.
John Griffiths Collection 57, 92, 93, 95, 98.
Hulton Picture Library 52, 61.
Illustrated London News 53, 54-55, 58, 96-97, 99, 132, 133, 134, 135, 136.
RFU Museum 94.
South West News 84, 85, 86, 87.
Billy Stickland 11, 14, 43, 100, 102, 105, 106 (top), 107, 108, 109 (top), 113, 114, 115 (top).
Surrey Comet 62, 63.
Topham 56, 59, 60, 139.